INSIGHT GUIDES

Nepal

Directed and Designed by Hans Höfer
Produced and Edited by Lisa Choegyal

APA
PUBLICATIONS

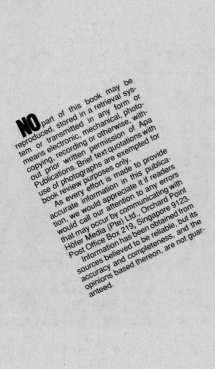
Nepal

First Edition

ABOUT THIS BOOK

Welcome to *Insight Guide Nepal*. A team of experts familiar with all aspects of life in Nepal have combined, under the leadership of **Lisa Choegyal**, to produce the most authoritative and complete guide yet to the mountains and jungles of Nepal. The cultural monuments of the Kathmandu Valley are covered in detail but the book focuses on Nepal as a whole, travelling the trade trails and exploring the pilgrimage routes of the highest mountains in the world. The travel section surveys the peaks, explains the treks, and helps you enjoy the wildlife of the Terai. The diverse terrain of Nepal has something memorable to offer every visitor.

Lisa Choegyal has been a resident in Nepal since 1974 and is a Director of the Tiger Mountain group which arranges the best of adventure travel in Asia. She travels extensively throughout the country and is author of *Insight Pocket Guide: Nepal* and producer of the *Cityguide: Kathmandu Valley*. In addition to editing and organising this volume, she contributed the section on festivals, Kathmandu Valley and Travel Tips, and commissioned the rest from acknowledged Nepal authorities and experts.

The Right Staff

Wendy Brewer Fleming wrote the adventure tourism, trekking, hill stations, Pokhara and river running sections as well as gave Himalayan-sized assistance in planning, advising, organising and editing. Fleming is a writer and trek leader and was for three years editor of *Nepal Traveller* magazine.

Sir Edmund Hillary, the world famous explorer and writer, contributed the first-person article on his experience with the Sherpa people. **Reinhold Messner** contributed the feature on what drives him to climb. Messner is the superstar of mountaineering who by October 1986 was the first to have scaled all the world's 8,000-meter giants.

Dr. Harka Bahadur Gurung, who wrote about geology and the Gurkhas, is one of Nepal's leading scholars and writers. Educated at the University of Edinburgh, he is a former Government minister and now has his own consultancy in Kathmandu.

The historical overview was written by **Charles Allen**, author of many books about the subcontinent, including his greatly acclaimed *Plain Tales from the Raj*. He and his brother, **Col. M.G. Allen** who wrote on fishing, were born and brought up in India.

Dor Bahadur Bista, Nepal's foremost anthropologist, contributed much of the section on the people of Nepal. **Father John K. Locke**, a Jesuit who has made a lifelong study of Hindu and Buddhist religions, wrote the piece on religion.

Charles Ramble, contributor of Natural Crossroads and the Yak and Shaman features, is a Kathmandu-based social anthropologist whose doctoral degree from Oxford University was for research conducted among Tibetan-speaking people in Nepal. He is currently Wildlife Director of Machan Wildlife Resort.

Kunda Dixit wrote the piece concerning the country's development and environmental dilemmas, Dixit is a leading Nepalese journalist based in the Philippines.

Choegyal

Fleming

Allen

O'Connor

Dixit

One of Britain's most experienced mountaineers and photographers, **Bill O'Connor** wrote the book *Trekking Peaks in Nepal*. He was the obvious person to contribute the Trekking Peak and 8,000-Meter Mountain sections and also some of his beautiful photographs.

World expert on the tiger, **Charles McDougal** has worked in Nepal since the 1960s. Wildlife Director for the Tiger Mountain group, he wrote the National Park and Jungle Safari sections. Mark Graham contributed the rare shot of the tiger in the wild.

Gisele Krauskopff, an anthropologist teaching at Paris University, worked among the unstudied Tharu people since 1975 and has published many articles and a book. She has a unique knowledge of and enthusiasm for the Nepal Terai and contributed the Tharu and Terai sections.

The features and pages involve some distinguished Nepal experts. **Elizabeth Hawley** is a journalist widely regarded as a one-woman Himalayan mountaineering institute. She is Executive Officer of Sir Edmund Hillary's Himalayan Trust and contributed the piece on Mallory and Irvine, interviewed Reinhold Messner and advised on all mountaineering aspects of the book.

David R. Shlim M.D. is medical director of the Himalayan Rescue Association and director of the CIWEC clinic in Kathmandu. His feature on problems at altitude is relevant to all trekkers. **Johan Reinhard** contributed the Shangrila legend. He has won awards for anthropology in the Himalaya and the Andes and specialises in mountain worship. **Frances Klatzel** has spent much of the last eight years in the Everest region creating the library and cultural centre at Thyangboche. **Maureen DeCoursey** wrote the page on the Gurung Hillwoman, drawn from her knowledge working for the Annapurna Conservation Area Project. **Frances Wall Higgins** introduced commercial mountain biking to Nepal and contributed a page on the subject.

Picture Perfect

Over twenty photographers combined to illustrate this book. **Galen Rowell**, the famous American climber and mountain photographer, contributed the backbone from his extensive collection. A frequent visitor to Nepal on mountaineering expeditions, he and his wife Barbara have produced works on Nepal and Tibet for *National Geographic*.

Less well-known names whose outstanding talent give this volume its atmosphere include **Devendra Basnet, Kevin Bubriski, Alain Evrard, Charles Gay, Thomas Laird, Craig Lovell, Gary McCue** and **Jock Montgomery**. All have lived in Nepal for months at a time and most are writers, photographers and trek leaders. They share a knowledge and passion for the country reflected in their work.

Special thanks must go to **Col. Jimmy Roberts**, founder of the trekking industry and Mountain Travel Nepal. He looked over the trekking sections and his advice, as always, was invaluable.

The late **Desmond Doig** was much missed but his Yeti feature lives on. Of great assistance were the **Ministry of Tourism, Tiger Mountain** group, **A.V. Jim Edwards, T.B. Shrestha, Manorma Mathai Moss** and **Tenzin Choegyal**.

—APA Publications

Ramble

Krauskopff

Rowell

Laird

Montgomery

CONTENTS

HISTORY AND PEOPLE

23 Sacred Himalaya

31 In the Beginning

39 Where Men and Mountains Meet

51 And Then There was Man

61 *Gurkhas: Bravest of the Brave*

67 Centre of the Universe

77 Festivals for all Seasons

82 Shamans: Healers of the High Himalaya

87 Natural Crossroads

92 *National Parks, Wildlife Reserves
    and Protected Areas*

99 The Fragile Mountain

EXPLORING THE KATHMANDU VALLEY

119 Cultural Crossroads

The Great Cities
121 Kathmandu – The Nation's Capital
130 Patan – The Beautiful City
135 Ridgetop Kirtipur
136 Bhaktapur – A Medieval Marvel

The Great Shrines
145 Buddhist Stupas
146 Vishnu Temples
149 Shiva Shrines
150 Other Sacred Spots

153 Great Natural Valley Sites

BEYOND THE VALLEY

163 **Playground of the Gods**

168 *Mountain Biking in Nepal*

172 **West Nepal**

180 **Annapurna Himal**

184 *A Day in the Life of a
Gurung Hillwoman*

193 **Central Nepal**

199 **Hikes in the Kathmandu Valley**

205 **Yaks: Life Support Systems**

208 **Yetis: Fiends in High Places?**

213 **Everest and the East**

220 *Gompas: Sherpa Monasteries
of Solu Khumbu*

231 **Trekking Peaks**

241 *Everest: Climbing to the Roof
cf the World*

243 **Vanishing into Thin Air:
Problems at High Altitude**

246 *Because It Is There:
The Legend of Mallory and Irvine*

250 **Nepal's 8,000-Meter Mountains**

257 **Shangrila and the Hidden Valleys**

262 *A Tale of Two Mountaineers*

264 *Reinhold Messner:*
Why Does Man Climb?

266 *Sir Edmund Hillary:*
My Life with Sherpas

271 Viewpoints

276 *Mountain Flight of a Lifetime*

281 Pokhara Valley

285 River Rafting

287 *Sport Fishing in Nepal*

291 Jungle Safaris

297 *Tharu Tribes*

303 The Terai: Granary of Nepal

307 *Birthplace of Lord Buddha*

MAPS

119A Nepal
119B Kathmandu Valley
119C West Nepal
119D Annapurna Himal
119E Lantang Himal & East Nepal
119F Central & East Nepal
  294 Royal Chitwan National Park

TRAVEL TIPS

GETTING THERE
314 By Air
314 By Rail
315 By Road

TRAVEL ESSENTIALS
315 Visas & Passports
316 Money Matters
316 Health
316 What to Wear
317 Customs

GETTING ACQUAINTED
317 Government & Economy
318 Time Zones
318 Calendars
319 Climate
319 Culture & Customs
320 Weights & Measures
321 Electricity
321 Business Hours
321 Holidays & Festivals
321 Religious Services

COMMUNICATIONS
321 Media
322 Postal Services
322 Telephone & Telefax

EMERGENCIES
322 Medical Services

GETTING AROUND
323 Maps
323 From the Airport
323 Domestic Travel
325 Public Transport
325 Private Transport
326 On Foot

WHERE TO STAY
326 Hotels & Lodges

FOOD DIGEST
332 What to Eat
332 Where to Eat
334 Drinking Notes

THINGS TO DO
334 Trekking
341 River Trips
342 Jungle Safaris
342 Mountain Biking

NIGHTLIFE
343 Cultural Shows
343 Movies
343 Gambling

SHOPPING
344 What to Buy
345 Where to Buy

SPORTS
346 Participant

PHOTOGRAPHY
346 Useful Tips

LANGUAGE
347 Nepali

FURTHER READING
347

USEFUL ADDRESSES
352 Royal Nepalese Missions Overseas
354 Foreign Missions
354 International Organisations
355 Airlines
355 Travel Agencies & Operators
355 Trekking Agencies
355 River Trip Operators

"In a hundred ages of the gods I could not tell thee of the glories of the Himalaya."

Cradled amongst the highest mountains in the world, it is no wonder that Nepal has come to be known as the kingdom where deities mingle with mortals.

Close to a billion people revere the Himalaya as sacred. These include followers of two of the world's major religions, Buddhism and Hinduism. Nowhere on earth does a mountain range figure so prominently in the religious beliefs of such a large and diverse population. The mountains are considered the dwelling place of deities and saints, and for some they are the very embodiment of the gods themselves.

Abode of the Gods: Sherpa artists depict Mount Everest, the highest point on earth, as the goddess Miyal Langsangma, one of the Five Long-Life Sisters. Makalu embodies a fierce guardian deity and Kangchenjunga is worshipped in a ceremony in which the god so named appears as a masked dancer. Gauri Shanker is the home of Shiva and his consort Parvati, Ganesh Himal is named for the elephant-headed god and Annapurna is the goddess of plenty.

Such beliefs date back thousands of years and feature in the oldest legends and epics. Mountain worship by primitive tribes predates the established religions. It is not difficult to perceive why. Mountains influence weather and are the sources of rivers, they affect the welfare of all who live in their shadow. They unite the earth and the sky and are believed to be the guardians of the land, people and animals within their domain.

Even today a number of Himalayan peaks are still not open to climbing expeditions, preserved as holy places. Whereas mountaineers see only the physical dangers, the villagers have to worry about the long-term consequences of angering the gods. Not only can they cause accidents on the mountain but they may provoke regional catastrophes such as illness, floods and avalanches. Everest expeditions regularly make offerings and burn juniper incense to appease the goddess before attempting a climb.

The Nepalese people live close to their gods. Truth no less colourful than fiction makes Nepal one of the world's most incredible countries, a geographical wonder, an ethnological conundrum.

Diverse Heritage: None can fail to be impressed by the diversity of the land that comprises Nepal. The flat, lush plains of the lowland Terai, the Siwalik (Churia) Hills swathed in hard-wood jungles, the ochre-red farmlands of the Inner Terai, the plunging flanks of the Mahabharat range, the fertile emerald Valley of Kathmandu, the deep gorges of turbulent grey-green rivers, and layer upon layer of

Preceding pages: Tharu women from the Terai of Nepal; Cholatse in the Everest region of Nepal; King Bupathindra Malla surveys the glory he created in Bhaktapur Durbar Square; soldiers serving in the Royal Nepal army are decorated for bravery; enjoying a *hookah* in a hill village. Left, Buddhist *lama* high in the Sherpa country of east Nepal.

foothills blued by distance. Beyond, the white Himalaya reach far above the clouds along the northern horizon. Within a single day one can fly past Everest and its neighbouring summits, pause amidst the palaces and temples of the Kathmandu Valley, then descend through the terraces of the middle hills to the plains and ride elephants through tropical jungle, inhabited with wild tigers.

This is the home of 19 million Nepalis. A rectangle 885 kilometers (553 miles) long and averaging 160 kilometers (100 miles) from north to south, Nepal bends to follow the curve of the central Himalaya. A country the size of Austria and Switzerland combined, Nepal's people, their languages and customs are as diverse as the terrain. From mountain to valley, plateau to plain, ethnic groups vary as much as the climate.

As many as 50 distinct languages and dialects have been identified and there are over 36 recognised different ethnic groups, each with their own cultural identity. The climate ranges from the nival waste of snow and ice above the alpine zone, to the humid, tropical lowland plains. The prevailing pattern of Hinduism to the south and Buddhism to the north is interwoven with Tantrism, animist rites and shamanistic practices. Both major religions co-exist in most of the country but they come together in the Kathmandu Valley to merge into a homogeneous and sophisticated civilisation.

"A Root Between Two Stones": Legends traditionally told the Nepalis all they needed to know about their origins, attributing unknown beginnings to heroes and gods. Swayambhunath was formerly a blue flame in a sacred lotus flower, floating on a pristine turquoise lake that became the Kathmandu Valley when drained by Manjushri's sword, creating present-day Chobar gorge.

Over the centuries, the history of Nepal encompasses waves of settlers who penetrated the mountain barrier from the north or the fever-infested southern jungles. A bewildering variety of people of Tibeto-Burmese and Indo-Aryan stock spread through the hills, plateaus and valleys of central Nepal. It was not uncommon for warring Himalayan principalities to invite help from an Indian or Tibetan prince, whose entourage would leave its mark on their adopted land.

Pilgrims, travellers and traders congregated, often for many months, in the clement surroundings of the Kathmandu Valley whilst waiting for passes to clear or swamps to dissipate. The genius of the indigenous Newar craftsmen was patronised by neighbouring admirers and the artisans themselves were exported along with their gilding, metalwork, woodcarving and stonework. The Chinese pagoda roof is said to have its origins and inspiration in the temple roof structures of Kathmandu.

Nepal is the world's only Hindu kingdom. It was first united by King Prithvi Narayan Shah of tiny Gorkha who subdued over 60 feuding states and principalities in the late 18th century and founded

Left, Seto Machhendra is paraded annually in a huge chariot through the streets of Kathmandu.

the current Shah dynasty.

He described his new kingdom as "a root between two stones", referring to Nepal's precarious position squeezed between the vastness of Tibet and China to the north and India to the south. Such a land, precariously strategic and beset by the disadvantage of being landlocked, is truly a slender root between two massive stones. This fact is cause for as many political headaches amongst today's rulers as it was for Prithvi Narayan Shah himself. Emerging at the end of the 20th century into a new-found constitutional democracy from the confines of a formerly feudal-based tradition, foreign relations are not Nepal's only political problem today.

Roof of the World: Except for the narrow strip of Terai plain along its southern boundary and the temperate valleys spread across its middle, the country is entirely mountainous. More than a quarter of Nepal's land area is over 3,000 meters (10,000 feet) in altitude.

This stupendous mountain pedestal includes eight of the earth's fourteen 8,000 meter (26,250 feet) mountains either within or on its borders, and eight of the ten highest mountains in the world: Everest, Kangchenjunga, Lhotse, Makalu, Cho Oyu, Dhaulagiri, Manaslu and Annapurna.

The highest mountain in the world is Mount Everest, which bestrides the Nepal-Tibet border in the east of the country. It is known to Nepalis as Sagarmatha (Mother of the Universe) and in Tibet as Chomolungma (Mother Goddess). Named after George Everest, a British surveyor-general in late 19th Century India, the highest point on earth was eventually climbed on 29th May, 1953 by Sir Edmund Hillary of New Zealand and Tenzing Norgay Sherpa of India.

Some of the high passes along the northern border with Chinese Tibet remain perpetually frozen. The snow-line varies between 5,000 and 6,000 meters (16,400 feet and 19,700 feet) descending lower during winter storms. Deep river valleys incise across the range to fall rapidly to the lower valleys. The youngest range of mountains in the world is still purported by geologists to be moving and growing, a fact attested to by earthquakes and subterranean tensions.

In the last decade, age-old patterns are altering as Nepal develops a measure of mobility, communications and political awareness. King Birendra Bir Bikram Shah Dev may not be recognised by all as an infallible reincarnation of the Hindu god Vishnu. The younger generation of the capital, Kathmandu, may be in danger of discarding individual cultural identity in favour of a drab national unity, flavoured with Western influence.

But if the Kathmandu Valley has long been considered to be Nepal, Nepal is by no means only Kathmandu. The hills and valleys of the hinterland, beneath the protecting peaks inhabited by the Himalayan gods, will long nurture the magnificent diversity and rich heritage to be discovered in Nepal.

Right, pilgrims beneath the sacred peak of Numbur bathe in the Dudh Kunda lake, Solu Khumbu.

The ancient conception of the Himalaya is one of utter immanence, the eternal home of the gods. It was an object of awe and devotion and not for men to enquire and fathom. However, a reflection on the genesis of the *shaligram* ammonite, the black fossil revered by the Hindus as an embodiment of Vishnu, leads to a geological past far beyond the age of man. The making of the ammonite fossil is related to the initial emergence of the Himalayan heights from the depths of a sea in the beginning of time.

The Collision of Continents: It was only seven decades ago that Alfred Wegener first postulated the theory of Continental Drift. The continents as we know them today were said to have broken off from a single land mass some hundreds of millions of years ago and "drifted" apart, riding on underlying plastic materials. Though discussions persist as to the actual cause and extent of the drift, modern geotechniques have reaffirmed the movement of continents, or plates, within the Theory of Plate Tectonics.

It is now largely accepted that the Himalaya were formed as a result of the collision of two large continental plates, the Indian subcontinent and Eurasia, in a process that began as early as 130 million years ago at the time when reptiles and dinosaurs roamed the earth. Having split off from a much larger southern continent called Gondwanaland - from which also came Australia, Antarctica, Africa and parts of South America - the Indian subcontinent travelled 4,400 kilometers (2,700 miles) northwards at an estimated rate of 20-25 centimeters (8-10 inches) per year and began colliding with the northern land mass, called Laurasia, approximately 50-60 million years ago.

The Tethys Sea: Studies of rock layers have been used to reconstruct the origins of the Himalaya, suggesting early periods of alternating subsidence and uplift of the earth's

surface. An extensive sea existed in the region where the Himalaya now rise, stretching right across the southern margin of Eurasia wedged between Laurasia and Gondwana. The sea, known as the Tethys, came into being some 250 million years ago during the Late Palaeozoic era, when the first reptiles appeared, and dried up gradually about 40-50 million years ago, when mammals came into being. Some scientists now think that the Tethys was actually a series of seas that repeatedly subsided, were uplifted and drained away with the passing of a number of land fragments set adrift from Gondwana which followed each other on a collision course into the northern Asian continent.

During this time, almost all of the now highly elevated areas between India and Central Asia were invaded by the Tethys Sea. Sinking and widening of the earth's surface commenced around 200 million years ago. It is believed that subsequent rising of the sub-surface brought the sea to a shallow level towards the Lower Cretaceous (110-135 million years ago). By 40 to 65 million years ago, the bottom had risen so much as to cause the water to spill over and

Preceding pages: sunrise over the Annapurna Himal of west Nepal. Left, ammonite fossils from the ancient Tethys Sea in the Kali Gandaki valley. Above, glaciers and river gorges (this one in the Annapurna area) have forged the Himalaya.

flood much of the surrounding land. This deluge was followed by the ultimate dissolution of the Himalayan sea, as evident by the fact that all later rock types found within the Himalaya (except those in localised basins) were laid down above water.

Thus, the rising of the Tethys Sea was primarily due to the build up of marine sediments, accumulating to great thicknesses of over 4,500 meters (15,000 feet) over a period of some 200 million years. Earlier, however, during the Jurassic and late Cretaceous era (70-80 to 195 million years ago), upheavals created some minor submarine ridges and valleys, accompanied by the appearance of volcanoes and subterra-

third Himalayan uplift was followed by a dormant period, coinciding with the Ice Age, when these first Himalayan chains were eroded down to form the Siwalik hills to the south. Siwalik deposits consist of coarse boulder conglomerates, 1,000 to 1,500 meters (3,000 to 5,000 feet) thick.

The fourth sequence in the uplift of the Himalaya occurred about two million years ago when older layers of rock were overthrust onto the deposits of the Siwaliks. This over-riding is well demarcated by the fault plane called the "main boundary thrust". The fifth and final upheaval ensued during the Pleistocene period, one to two million years ago, a time of much glacial activity when the

nean bodies of molten rock.

The Himalaya are Born: These upheavals were the first spasms of the birth of the Himalaya, which actually took place in a series of stupendous periods of uplift punctuated by intervals of comparative quiescence. A second upheaval occurred in the Upper Eocene (38-45 million years ago), raising the primary ridges and basins of the Tethys Sea into mountain ranges with intervening shallow marshes and large river valleys. It was, however, the intense mountain-building epoch of the mid-Miocene (seven to 26 million years ago) that created the major structure of the present-day Himalaya. This

progenitors of man were stirring. Its impact was felt most in the lower hills of the Himalaya where layers of rock were pushed up as much as 2,000 meters (6,000 feet).

Today's Tensions and Earthquakes: Ever since the first collision of continents, the Himalayan region has been subjected to compression, contortion, elevation and denudation. The area is still in the process of adjustment: the Indian subcontinent continues to push into Asia at a rate of about two inches (five centimeters) per year, as substantiated by the frequency of large slips along major faultlines beneath the Himalaya causing periodic earthquakes, as well as by more localized geologic events. In fact, most geologists agree that the Himalaya is still rising, noting more recent (Pliocene) overthrusting in the foothills and a 50-degree tilt of rock layers in the western Himalaya. Kathmandu lake deposits which now dip northwards were uplifted 200 meters (600 feet) over the last 200,000 years. The present rate of uplift is difficult to tell as accurate measurements have only been made over the last hundred years.

Back to the Sea: At the same time, the Himalaya are wearing down, as all young mountains do. The monsoon rains pound at their sides, and constant freezing and thawing cracks the rocks which cause them to

it scoops out a rounded valley, a cirque, which defines the mountains' ridges in bowls and sharp rims. From its terminus, a milky stream runs thick with finely ground sediments which will eventually wash all the way down to the Ganges, returning once-submarine deposits back to the sea.

Mountain Geography: But for the narrow strip of plain along Nepal's southern border, and temperate valleys spread across its middle, the country is entirely mountainous.

The northern part of the country is characterised by towering ice and snow ranges with occasional sparse valleys. This is the Himalayan or mountain region of the country, a part of Nepal conspicuous for its extreme

shed their outer layers. Although glacial fields are limited, they more than any constant force chisel away at the peaks and carve away the valleys. Season upon season of snow accumulates and is compressed into ice to depths of several hundred meters. The sheer weight shoves the glacier's lowest edge down the mountain, scraping away debris from the sides and bottom. At the top,

Left, Mount Everest from Kala Pattar showing the great Khumbu icefall. **Above**, wildly folded sedimentary rock high on Nuptse, photographed from 7,000 meters (24,000 feet) on Everest.

altitude and wild terrain. The highest ranges are crowned by jagged peaks. Ice-scooped basins found at lower elevations indicate a much wider glacial provenance in the past.

Mountain relief is asymmetrical, with rock strata inclined to the north, leaving steep south faces. The south-tending spurs of the main range are covered with temperate forests lower down and confine steep valleys marked with occasional waterfalls. Thunderstorms are frequent and winter frosts limit agriculture. Nevertheless, potatoes are grown to 4,000 meters (13,100 feet) and barley even higher.

North of the main range, the prospect is

much more desolate with bare mountain slopes and undulating valley bottoms filled with rock debris and sparse vegetation in sheltered corners. This mountain region is a marginal area for human settlement and hence man's influence on the landscape is minimal. Summers are short, winters severe and dry with high snowfall, low temperatures and strong winds.

In the northwest of the country a fourth, trans-Himalayan range defines the boundary between Nepal and Tibet. Peaks of 6,000 to 7,000 meters (19,700 to 23,000 feet) lie about 35 kilometers (22 miles) north of the main Himalaya; their relief is less rugged, and wind-eroded landforms predominate.

sected by numerous river valleys. While the smaller valleys make narrow, steep defiles, the larger ones have an easy gradient and a wide open character. The main north-south valleys and their upper tributary extensions make deep indentations in the middle hill topography and these low valleys have numerous old river terraces indicating changing geologic or climatic conditions at the time of alluvial deposits. Landslides and landslips are common and tributary streams, overloaded with washed-down materials, unload alluvial cones at their termini.

The mild subtropical climate and adequate rainfall have made the midland area a favourable zone for agricultural settlement.

Here elevated *bhot* valleys - broad with open profiles and arid climate - are reminiscent of Tibet, particularly where the Himalayan rainshadow blocks out the monsoon rains.

Middle Hills: Below the Himalaya, running in a similar west-northwest to east-southeast direction 90 kilometers (56 miles) south of the great rise is the Mahabharat range, reaching elevations between 1,500 and 2,700 meters (4,900 and 8,900 feet). These are referred to as the sub-Himalaya.

The middle hill region, also called the *pahar*, extends between the Mahabharat and the high Himalaya. Its characteristic landforms are low hills and sinuous ridges, dis-

Farmers have cleared vast hillsides of trees for cultivation, spoiling the natural landscape. The typical scenery of the middle hill country is flights of terraced fields carved out of steep slopes.

The clement Kathmandu Valley falls in this belt. The moderate climate permits three harvests a year and small plantings in between. Summer maximums are about 30°C (86°F) and mean winter temperatures about 10°C (50°F). Winters are sometimes frosty, but are dry and snowless, while summer monsoons bring substantial rain. Visitors are often surprised to learn that Kathmandu's latitude -about 27°40'North - is the same as that of Florida and Kuwait, and slightly south of New Delhi.

The Lowland Landscape: The area south of the Mahabharat hills is generally known as the Terai. Despite the intervening Siwalik range, this southern region of Nepal is virtually flat, a finely graded alluvial plain overlain with silt and sand. Twenty-five to forty kilometers (15 to 25 miles) broad within the Nepalese border, the recumbent Terai is a northern extension of India's vast Ganges plain.

The Siwalik (sometimes called the Churia) range stands out conspicuously from the swampy lowlands. They rise to heights of 750 to 1,500 meters (2,450 to 4,900 feet),

or Inner Terai valleys between the Siwalik and Mahabharat hills. These longitudinal valleys have been formed mainly by the depositions from the slopes of the enclosing Mahabharat and Siwalik ranges.

Summers are hot in the Terai and the *dun*, with temperatures often exceeding 38°C (100°F). Winters are considerably cooler, with temperatures down to 10°C (50°F). Rainfall comes primarily in the June-to-September monsoon, heaviest in the east.

The Impact of Man: Man attempts to adapt himself to the natural environment and in the process leaves his imprint on the landscape. The Terai's natural environment has considerably changed over the last decade through

higher in west Nepal corresponding to the elevated Terai which stands an average of 180 meters (600 feet) above sea level in the west compared with 90 meters (300 feet) in the east. Elsewhere the Siwaliks have been much reduced in height and even appear as isolated hillocks. Their dry, immature soils support only a sparse population.

At a slightly higher elevation to the Terai plain, but with similar vegetation, lie the *dun*

Left, a remote monastery is protected by trees in a valley sculpted with terraces in east Nepal. **Above**, ferns and leaves flourish in the summer monsoon.

the agency of man. The southern strip of the Terai plain has been transformed into an extensive belt of farms and new settlers have made deep in-roads into the area by clearing forest and draining marshes.

While harsh conditions dominate in the mountain region, in the middle hill areas man has again left his mark by removing natural vegetative cover, thereby hastening soil erosion. This depletion of a critical natural resource is reflected in the increasing migration of farmers to the Terai.

It is no wonder that the Nepalese deify the imposing mountains that divide them, and sanctify the fertile rivers that unite them.

WHERE MEN AND MOUNTAINS MEET

This awesome mountainous land was named by the ancients *Himarant* or *Himalaya*, the "Abode of Snow". Set deep in the mountains, between the Great Himalayan Range and the lower Mahabharat, was a lake. Nepalese legends speak of an island on this lake upon which grew a blue lotus containing the eternal flame of the Primordial Buddha. Manjushri, a manifestation of the Buddha, came to worship here and, to make access easier for pilgrims, he cut a passage through the Mahabharat hills and so drained the lake. A fertile valley was revealed, men settled here to farm and build cities and this became Nepal. Swayambhunath hill and its famous stupa on the summit mark the site of the original lotus island. Chobar Gorge, through which the Bagmati River drains the Kathmandu Valley, is where the Bodhisattva made his cut through the mountains.

Early Kingdoms: The first kingdoms of Nepal were confined to the Kathmandu Valley. Other centres of civilisation developed in what is now the Terai, Nepal's southern plains country. One of these was at Lumbini where in 543 B.C. was born the "Light of Asia", Prince Siddhartha Gautama, son of a local ruler, who achieved enlightenment to become the Buddha.

Of Kathmandu Valley the Nepalese chronicles detail the rise and fall of successive dynasties of rulers: the Gopalas, the Kiratis, the Licchavis. In 637 A.D. the Chinese pilgrim, Hsuan Chuang, found its inhabitants to be of a "hard nature" but with many talents. These were the Newars, still the majority population in the Valley today. Even 1400 years ago their artistic and mercantile skills were evident:

"The houses are of wood, painted and sculpted. The people are fond of bathing, of dramatic performances, of astrology and of blood sacrifices. Irrigation, carefully and skilfully applied, makes the soil rich. Both Buddhism and Brahmanism (Hinduism)

flourish in the main temples, which are wealthy and well supported. Commerce prospers and trade is well organised."

Already Nepal had built up profitable trading links with its powerful neighbours to the north and south, acting as middleman between two strong cultures, and in the process building up a distinctive culture of its own. This Nepalese culture came into full flower during the extended dynasty of the Malla kings. The first Malla came to power in 1200 A.D., the last was deposed in 1769. Greatest of the Malla kings was Jayasthiti Malla, who set late-14th century Nepal on the map of Asia as a prosperous, well-ordered nation. However three generations later, in 1482, the country was divided among three Malla brothers and a sister. Each became ruler of one of the four Valley towns - Kathmandu, Bhaktapur, Banepa and Lalitpur (now Patan) - and each established an independent ruling dynasty. Rivalry between these city-states led to nearly three centuries of vigorous artistic competition as the Malla kings vied to outdo each other in splendour. Newari artistry in temple and palace building, wood-carving, metal working and scroll-painting transformed Kathmandu Valley into one of the world's richest repositories of art and architecture.

Feuding amongst themselves weakened the political supremacy of the Mallas in the region and in the surrounding hills other local rulers began to bid for power. The Muslim conquest of Northern India had driven a number of Rajput princes and their followers into the mountains. In 1559 one of these chieftains, Druvya Shah, seized the hill-fort of Gorkha, three days' march west of Kathmandu. From this stronghold his descendants gradually extended their authority over the *paharis* or hill-people of the Chaubasi Raj, the "24 Kingdoms" of central Nepal, until Prithvi Narayan Shah invaded Kathmandu Valley with his Gorkha troops. After a prolonged campaign lasting 10 years, by 1769 his conquest was complete, the Malla kings were dethroned and the Shahs became the new rulers of Nepal. His successors continued his policy of expansion after his death at the age of 52 in 1775. In effect,

Preceding pages: Chandra Shamsher Jung Bahadur Rana, ruler of Nepal in the early 20th century, flanked by his family. Left, King Prithvi Narayan Shah of Gorkha, founder of modern Nepal.

King Prithvi Narayan Shah laid the foundations of the present day Kingdom of Nepal.

War and Peace: Nepal then entered a period of conquest that pushed its boundaries west along the Himalaya as far as Kashmir and eastwards to Sikkim. The Nepalese next laid claim to the fertile plains to the south, where the authority of the Mogul Emperors had long been in decline. But here they came up against a rival power, the British East India Company, that was also expanding to fill the political vacuum. Diplomacy failed and in 1814 Nepal and Britain went to war. The East India Company sent four armies into the hills. Two failed to make any headway, one was repulsed and the fourth broke the main Nepal army after a hard contest.

A peace-treaty was signed in 1816 at Segauli, initiating a friendship that benefited both parties. Nepal secured her frontiers and diverted Britain's empire-building ambitions elsewhere, while the British gained a staunch ally. It was from Nepal's defeated army that volunteers came forward to form the first of the famous Gurkha regiments that to this day still serve the British Crown.

Only one feature of the "Treaty of Friendship" really irked the Nepalis: a clause requiring the Government of Nepal to accept a British Resident in Kathmandu. The Nepalis had always been fierce protectors of their independence and had never made strangers welcome, unless they came as pilgrims. Two European Jesuits had passed safely through Kathmandu in 1661 while travelling from China to India, but a party of Capuchin missionaries who followed met with disaster when it was discovered that they had come to win converts. Successive British Residents scarcely fared any better. The British Residency was deliberately sited on waste land said to be haunted by evil spirits - and its human occupants found themselves virtual prisoners with their movements, even within the Valley, severely restricted.

Nepal's self-imposed isolation from the outside world was greatly intensified when, in 1846, an army officer named Jung Bahadur Rana took advantage of a crisis meet-

ing being held in the government armoury, known as the Kot, to massacre virtually everybody present. The king was spared, but Jung Bahadur took over the reins of power as Prime Minister and Commander-in-Chief - and ensured that after his death both posts would be inherited by a member of his own family. The Shahs remained as venerated monarchs, but it was the Ranas who ruled.

For a century the Ranas stuck to a policy of despotic self-quarantine. Writing in 1928, the journalist Percival Landon estimated that no more than 120 English and ten other Europeans had entered Kathmandu Valley before him. Of those who had entered, none had been permitted to set foot in the sur-

rounding hills except when entering or leaving Nepal, although a privileged few had been allowed to join their Rana hosts in tiger and rhinoceros shoots in the Terai. Trade links with British India were strictly controlled and what few goods were imported, chiefly to grace the palaces of the Ranas, had to be carried in on the backs of porters, since no roads were allowed to be developed.

Trade and Exploration: Only along Nepal's borders with Tibet were the local communities permitted to maintain their links with their neighbours. This border area lies north of the Great Himalayan Range and is the home of tribal groups of Tibetan stock

Left, hunts with royal invitees were popular in the early 1900s and huge "bags" of tiger and rhinoceros were recorded. **Above**, a portrait in the National Museum of Bhimsen Thapa, an early prime minister.

known collectively as Bhotia. They include the famous mountain guides of Solu Khumbu, the Sherpas, yak farmers and traders settled in the upper reaches of the Dudh Kosi in the east, who in the summer months traded into Tibet by way of the 5,716 meter (18,753 foot) Nangpa La pass. Another notable northern community is the Buddhist people of Lo or Mustang at the headwaters of the Kali Gandaki in western Nepal, who traditionally traded grain for salt across the Mustang Pass. Two other crossing points into Tibet served as traditional conduits for trade, both river passes: the Khirong La on the Trisuli River north of Kathmandu, and the Kuti La on the upper Sunkosi, the main

giri massif, the world's seventh highest mountain. For the next 30 years the map-makers of the Survey of India concentrated on mapping India using a system of triangulation devised by the Surveyor-General of India, Sir George Everest. After his retirement in 1843 interest once more returned to the Himalayan barrier.

By 1852 the two great cornerstones at the far reaches of Nepal, the 8,586 meter (28,169 foot) Kangchenjunga massif in the east and Gurla Mandhata (7,728 meters, 25,355 feet) in the Nalakankar Himal in the west, had been accurately plotted, but the 800 kilometers (500 miles) of mountains and valleys between these two points lay unmapped and

trade route to Lhasa and therefore the most closely guarded.

The first European to grasp the extraordinary nature of Nepal's mountains was the great geographer and map-maker James Rennell, who in 1788 observed that the highest snow peaks could be seen from the Indian plains at a distance of 240 kilometers (150 miles). When it was declared that some of the peaks might be as high as 8,000 meters (26,250 feet) there was disbelief but in 1811 a very prominent peak in west Nepal, observed from four survey stations in the Indian plains, was calculated to be 8,167 meters (26,795 feet) high. This was the Dhaula-

tantalisingly out of reach. The best that the Survey of India could do was to take theodolite bearings from the plains and compute them to produce a rough map. In 1849 bearings were taken from six different stations on a peak in east Nepal, identified only as Peak XV. Three years passed before the day when a computation clerk rushed into the office of the Surveyor-General with the news that he had "discovered the highest mountain in the world."

Everest Discovered: Once the first figure of 8,840 meters (29,002 feet) for the height of Peak XV had been verified, strenuous efforts were made to find the mountain's local name. This proved fruitless, with the unfortunate result that in 1865 Peak XV was named Mount Everest by the Survey of India. Unfortunate, because years later it was found that Everest did have a Tibetan name, Chomolungma, which has been translated variously as "Mother Goddess", "Lady Cow" or "The Mountain So High That No Bird Can Fly Over It". The official Nepalese name for Peak XV is Sagarmatha, which honours the demon-slaying King Sagar of Hindu legend and reminds the world that Nepal is a Hindu kingdom that reveres its snow-peaks as the home of the gods. The true altitude of Mount Everest, 8,848 meters (29,028 feet), was later established by im-

to Kathmandu so that Everest could be finally identified from the surrounding hills, and not until 1949 was the first climbing party permitted to enter any great distance into the country.

The Pundits: But if official visitors were forbidden to explore Nepal, what was to stop unofficial visitors from venturing in disguise? In 1863 the Survey of India hit upon the idea of using Himalayan traders to act as their surveyors. Two such men, Nain Singh and Mani Singh from Kumaon Himalaya, were the first of these explorer-spies, later known as the Pundits. They were trained for two years, given a disguise and then sent into the Himalaya with their survey instruments

proved measuring techniques, which accounts for the discrepencies in many peaks' altitudes now officially standardised by the Nepal government.

What is remarkable is that from the time of its "discovery" in 1852 Everest was to remain inviolate for another full century. Only in 1903 was an officer of the Survey of India permitted by the Rana government to come

Left, the oldest inscription in the Kathmandu Valley, dated 467 AD, is engraved in stone at Changu Narayan. **Above**, a Malla king honors Indra in a 15th century fresco at the Palace of Bhaktapur.

hidden in secret compartments in their luggage. Lhasa was their main target but Nepal was their means of entry into Tibet. In March 1865 Nain Singh and Mani Singh crossed into Nepal and after a brief stay in Kathmandu attempted to enter Tibet by way of the Khirong La. Suspicious Nepalese customs officials detained them and searched their baggage without finding their instruments before sending them back to Kathmandu. The two then split up, Mani Singh heading west to attempt a crossing via Mustang while Nain Singh tried the Khirong La. Mani Singh failed but brought back a great deal of information about western Nepal. Nain Singh had better luck and returned to his base in India in July 1866 after an epic journey of 2,000 kilometers (1,200 miles).

These were the first of many journeys of exploration through forbidden territory made by Nain Singh, Mani Singh and their successors. The exploits of these brave men remained a closely guarded secret for some years and when accounts of their journeys were first revealed, their identities were concealed and details of their journeys withheld. The British were also anxious to preserve good relations with the Ranas, so very little was ever written about the "opening up" of Nepal by the Pundits, who would certainly have faced years of imprisonment or death

central section of Nepal. He first made his way eastward across the high country that drains into the Sunkosi river and up into Solu Khumbu to cross into Tibet over the Nangpa La. He then marched east for 160 kilometers (100 miles) before crossing back into Nepal by way of the Khirong La. The last section of this seven month survey - all of it paced out on foot by counted, measured steps and compass-bearings - took him down through the Gorkha region between Kathmandu and Pokhara.

Mountaineers and Pilgrims: Forbidden Nepal drew other trespassers besides the Pundits. The most secretive was probably an Englishman named Edmund Smyth who, as

had their spying been discovered.

As a result the name of Hari Ram, code-name "M.H." or "Number 9", is hardly known today. Yet this forgotten Pundit, also a Kumaoni, quite literally did more to put Nepal on the map than any other single individual. In 1871 he made the first circuit of eastern Nepal and the Everest region in a 1,300 kilometers (800 mile) route survey. Two years later he entered western Nepal from Kumaon and traversed the northern belt as far as the Kali Gandaki gorge, making a brief foray into Tibet before returning to follow the river down into India. Then, 14 years on, Hari Ram set out to survey the

Kumaon's first Education Officer, chose Nain Singh and Mani Singh for their new profession. Smyth's chief interests lay in mountaineering, exploring and hunting rather than his work. He made two illicit journeys over the Himalayan ranges and was probably the first Westerner to "climb" in the Himalaya, following his introduction to this new sport in the Alps in 1854. He left no record of his activities but a book of reminiscences published by a retired Forest Officer in 1902 gives away at least one of his secrets. It tells us that in 1864 Smyth led a totally unauthorised expedition through the north-western corner of Nepal and over a 6,000 meter (20,000 feet) snow pass for a spot of yak hunting in Tibet.

If Smyth was the most reticent of explorers, the aptly-named Henry Savage Landor was the most boastful. This English gentleman-cad bullied his way through the same corner of west Nepal in 1897 and after being beaten up by the Tibetan authorities was thrown out again. To round off his trip, all later enlarged upon in a lurid, two-volume best-seller, *In the Forbidden Land*, Savage Landor made a record-breaking ascent of a 7,000 meter (23,400 feet) Nepalese peak Mount Api, wearing his straw boater and carrying a malacca cane. Another more worthy trespasser into Nepalese territory,

a Tibetan monk. This highly eccentric traveller came in search of the original scriptures of Buddhism, which he believed he would find hidden in the monasteries of Nepal and Tibet. Lhasa was his goal, but beguiled by the austere charms of the upper Kali Gandaki valley, he lingered in Nepal for 15 months before moving on into Tibet. Kawaguchi's accounts of his adventures, later published as *Three Years in Tibet*, were dismissed as fiction when he returned to Japan. Nothing daunted, the monk gathered funds for a second journey, returning to Nepal in 1903. This time he came quite openly as a Japanese seeking Sanskrit texts. The Rana prime minister of the day, Chandra Shamsher,

the mountaineer Tom Longstaff, came that same way six years later and was not surprised to find that Landor's 7,000 meter climb had lost some 2,000 meters (6,500 feet) over the intervening years, Landor having never reached the summit.

Others trespassed with higher motives, most notably the Japanese Zen Buddhist monk Ekai Kawaguchi, who first entered Nepal in 1899 dressed in the maroon robes of

Left, demonstrators clashing with police on 6th April 1990 on Durbar Marg. **Above**, victory celebrations followed the lifting of the ban on political parties, 9th April 1990.

happened to be on a hunting trip in the Terai. Kawaguchi secured an audience with him and was given permission to proceed to Kathmandu Valley - only to find himself as restricted in his movements as any British Resident. A month later he was given his scriptures and escorted back across the border. In 1905 he returned for a third and last time to Kathmandu, living for ten months at the Buddhist centre of pilgrimage at Bodhnath, under the shadow of its great stupa. He was now a well-known and much respected figure - but remained as much a prisoner of the Ranas as before.

The Doors Open: Despite the major assistance in terms of fighting men and funds given to Britain and India by Nepal during the two World Wars, it was not until the last stages of World War Two that the Ranas began to relax their grip on the country. In 1944 King Tribhuvan, who had ascended to the throne as a minor in 1911, was at last able to visit India and Europe. He initiated contacts with progressive forces outside Nepal and in November 1950 put his demands for a return to constitutional monarchy to the Rana government. He then briefly sought refuge in India before returning to bring about a "palace revolution" on 18th February 1951 that overthrew the Ranas and reestablished the Shahs as the rulers of Nepal.

A cabinet drawn from the Nepalese Congress Party was formed to govern the country and for almost a decade a succession of cabinets and prime ministers came and went without providing the effective government that Nepal needed.

However, this return to modern rule at last allowed Nepal to open its doors to the outside world. Desperately needed development programmes were started. Roads, schools, hospitals and much else were built and, through stages, visitors were gradually welcomed.

In 1950 a French mountaineering expedition had been granted access to western Nepal, where with strong Sherpa support it made the first ascent of Annapurna I, at 8,091 meters (26,545 feet) the highest mountain yet climbed and the first 8,000 meter (26,250 foot) peak in the world to be successfully scaled. This set the pattern for future mountaineering expeditions. In 1951 a British expedition made the first reconnaissance of Mount Everest from the Nepal side, during which the large footprints of the elusive yeti were photographed for the first time. A Swiss party followed in 1952 and, although Raymond Lambert and Tenzing Norgay Sherpa passed the 8,500 meter (28,000 feet) mark, it was left to Edmund Hillary from New Zealand and the heroic Tenzing Norgay, then on his seventh expedition to Everest, to finally conquer the world's highest mountain in May 1953.

King Tribhuvan died in March 1955 and was succeeded by his son King Mahendra, who in December 1960 assumed direct rule while he drew up a new constitution based on his conviction that Western-style parliamentary democracy could not work in Nepal. In its place he instituted the Panchayat system, based on the traditional Hindu model of the five (*panch*) man village council. This provided for locally elected, non-party representation and government at ward, village, district and zone levels, as well as a National Panchayat assembly to ratify decisions taken by a Council of Ministers appointed by the King. On the death of King Mahendra in 1972, his Western-educated son, His Majesty King Birendra Bir Bikram Shah Dev, inherited the throne.

The youthful King Birendra amended the constitution in 1980, following a national referendum. Maintaining the single party system, the new constitution gave more powers to the assembly, who appointed the cabinet and the Prime Minister, though only with the endorsement of the King.

Nepal remains the only Hindu monarchy in the world but in April 1990 popular discontent, manifested by demonstrations and riots, forced King Birendra to lift the legal ban on political parties. An interim government was appointed to prepare a constitution and arrange elections that would introduce a truly democratic system to Nepal.

Above, Nepalese soldier. **Right**, the eyes of Swayambhunath.

46

AND THEN THERE WAS MAN

Nepal is a veritable mosaic of over thirty different ethnic groups with their unique languages, cultures and religions who have over the centuries penetrated and settled the hills and valleys of Nepal, coming from the north and south, east and west. Despite this diversity, Nepal has a tradition of harmony rather than conflict. Society here has always been accommodating to new ideas, new values and new peoples from afar.

In this land of ethnic elements as varied as its landscape, the principles of integration and synthesis were accepted from ancient times. The earliest distinguishable races were an intermixture of Khas and Kiratis with other immigrant groups. Today, a striking example of this amalgam of north and south, of Tibeto-Burman and Indo-Aryan stocks, are the Newars of Kathmandu Valley. Patronised by the ruling nobility, the genius of Newari artisans can be seen in the temples, palaces, *bahals* (monasteries) and *chowks* (courtyards) that constitute the man-made environment of the Valley today.

The Genius of the Newars: The original Newar settlements of the Valley and beyond reflect concern for the prudent use of valuable agricultural land. Often located along ridge spines, Newari houses clustered around sites of religious significance, expanding on the basis of the individual family's structure. Villages expanded laterally along these plateaus, leaving the more fertile low-lying areas for farming. In this way, organic wastes ultimately found their way to the farms, adding valuable nutrients to the soil.

The Gorkha invasion of 1768 brought a concept of nationhood into this ancient and traditional milieu. With the establishment of the capital of a united Nepal in Kathmandu, the tightly knit homogeneity of the Valley was interjected with new values. The Gorkha settlers' more independent family structure spilled over into the traditional urban precincts.

Preceding pages: an ethnic mosaic of women and children watch the Indrajatra festival. **Left,** Tamang women. **Above,** Konjo Chumbi, a Sherpa elder statesman from Khumjung village.

What one sees today in Kathmandu is precisely this mixture: a medieval township that finds itself in the midst of the 20th century, a blending of the essence of old Kathmandu with the effects of latter-day migration from outside the Valley.

In a valley where there are said to be more religious monuments than houses, it is sometimes difficult to tell the difference between the divine and the worldly. A Newari house can only be built with sacred permission, which must come prior to the foundation

laying ceremony and then again after the roofing of the house. The fire-baked bricks are prepared in the Valley, though not in the old wedge-shapes which give the palaces such a distinctive air. The intricately worked wood window frames and doorways are carved as lovingly as on any temple.

The extended family is the cornerstone of Newari society and acts as both a support and a refuge. From an early age, the individual learns how to fit within the social nucleus and how to relate to the clan and caste, through respect for relatives and patron deities. Joint families can include three generations with 30 or more members.

The Newari *guthi* is on a higher plane than the family but symbolizes a deep aspiration to community living. These brotherhoods maintain local temple and communal services, organise feasts, festivals and processions, arrange burials, maintain family sanctuaries, care for the ailing and elderly, and even assist in the collective preparation of fields. The *guthi* provides substantial advantages to its members and is indicative of the social rank and economic potential of each family. This institution, present in the Valley since Malla times, has been both a factor of social integration and a means of perpetuating cultural values and achievements.

From birth to death, special rites and celebrations mark the important events of a Newar's existence. One of the more colourful initiations is when the young girls are "married" to the god Narayan before they reach puberty, with all the symbolic rituals of a typical wedding. Although the human marriage will come later, it will technically be her second, thus ensuring that the girl will never become a widow and will also make divorce a mere formality.

In a country where death comes early, age is respected and celebrated. The old are venerated, and when a relative reaches the auspicious age of 77 years, seven months and seven days, there is a reenactment of the *pasni*, or rice-feeding ceremony that all children go through when they are seven months old.

When death finally comes, the deceased must be taken, often in the pre-dawn hours, to the cremation *ghats* by the riverside. The sons must walk three times around their parent's corpse, carrying the butter lamp that will be placed on the face of the deceased. As the priest sets the pyre ablaze, the dead person's relatives get their heads shaved and ritually purify themselves with a bath in the sacred river. The ashes are scattered in the river which flows into the sacred Ganges.

Elsewhere in Kathmandu, life goes on - in the streets, courtyards, temples and on the

rooftops. The city is in a transition: from the tight bonds of Newari tradition and customs of the old, to the metamorphosis of the concrete reality of the jet-age present.

Watch the faces of the Nepalese people at any busy intersection in Kathmandu and you will soon discover what a fascinating melting pot of Himalayan cultures the city is. When you leave the Valley to visit outlying regions, you will find dozens of isolated pockets of distinct peoples and cultures.

The Tamang "Horse Soldiers": Outside the Valley rim, and well beyond it, live the Tamangs. Tamang is derived from "horse soldiers" in the Tibetan language, and it is supposed that they descended from Tibetan cavalry. Today, they are mostly small farmers; some work as porters and craftsmen, especially in wicker work and carpentry. Their elaborate two-story stone-and-wood houses are clustered along cobbled streets.

Tamangs are often seen in the streets of Kathmandu carrying large *doko* (baskets) by headstraps supported on their foreheads. The men and boys dress in loincloths and long, usually black tunics; in winter, they wear short-sleeved sheep-wool jackets, frequently with a *khukri* knife thrust in the waistband. They are a familiar sight carrying their hand-made, grey, beige and white *rhadis* (flat-weave carpets) for sale from

have priests and deities, and variations in the rites appear to be minimal. Whereas a Buddhist walks to the left of a shrine and spins his prayer wheel clockwise, a Bon believer, a Bonpo, walks to the right and spins his prayer wheel counter-clockwise.

Like many of Nepal's peoples, the Tamangs retain *jhankris* (shamans) in addition to their *lamas* (priests). These *jhankris* conduct religious ceremonies for communal and individual well-being: their ritual procedures involve trance and possession to drive away spirits for the sick or dying, to recover lost souls, and to perform various seasonal agricultural rites, such as making sacrifices to ensure good crops. Not surprisingly, many

house to house. Women wear above-the-ankle saris of homemade cotton, and blouses adorned with ornaments and jewellery.

Tamangs are Lama Buddhists, as are most upper Himalayan peoples. They have *gompas* (monasteries) in every sizeable village. The gods, religious paintings and texts, festivals and ritual ceremonies are all of Tibetan style. Some northern peoples follow the Bon religion, generally considered the pre-Buddhist religion of Tibet; but both religions

Left, boy with prayer wheels at the Golden Temple in Patan. <u>Above</u>, a Brahman bride and groom marry in traditional style in Solu Khumbu.

of these shamanistic rites are quite similar to those once found among the peoples of Mongolia and Siberia.

Polygamy is not uncommon in the hills, even though the government has restricted it and family economics are a limiting factor. There is an ambivalent attitude regarding sexual activities, with money as a soothing influence. If a Tamang man abducts the wife of another, for example, the new husband compensates the ex-spouse with money. Adultery is also punishable by lesser fines.

Life on the World's Edge: The high Himalayan settlements of Tibetan-speaking peoples perch precariously on mountain

ledges and fragile slopes. Life here is a delicate balance of hard work and social frivolity, tempered by a culture deeply founded in ancient religious tradition.

The best known of the high-mountain peoples are the Sherpas, inhabiting central and eastern hill regions of Nepal. Although the name "Sherpa" has become synonymous with "mountain guide", it is only those in the Everest region who have achieved relative prosperity through guiding mountaineering expeditions and escorting trekking groups, with their families often running small hotels and teashops in their home villages.

The southern limits of these Himalayan regions - places like Phaplu, Junbesi, Tarkeghyang and Jomosom - are sometimes thought of as attractive, even romantic, examples of high-altitude settlements. Indeed, many are. But the extreme north and other communities on higher slopes are not very comfortable or prosperous. These border settlements are few and far between; interaction with other villages requires long journeys and much of the year is spent in temporary shelters as moving with the seasons to provide grazing for their animals.

Among the inhabitants of these hardy climes are the 7,000 to 8,000 people of Mustang. They live in oasis villages on a reddish-brown rock desert, fighting a constant bitter wind to farm grains and potatoes in sheltered plots.

The hard grind of daily life and subsistence survival in the high Himalaya is interrupted by seasons of feasts and festivals, marked by drinking, dancing and merrymaking. Most festivals are of a religious nature and centre around the temples and monasteries, with rites conducted by *lamas* and *jhankris*. These celebrations occur on the full-moon days of May, June, July, August and November. They include the Dumje and Mani Rimdu rites of the Sherpas of Solu Khumbu; the Yartung festival of Muk-ti-nath; and the Dyokyabsi fest of Mustang.

The Clever Thakalis: Among the most interesting northern peoples of Nepal are the Thakalis. Residing in the upper Kali Gandaki river region, astride a seam of cultures, languages, ethnic groups, climatic conditions and historic traditions that are worlds apart from one another. Over several centuries, the Thakalis have successfully integrated Lamaism and Hinduism into their own colourful faith, and have mastered the arts of trade and commerce to emerge as perhaps the most successful entrepreneurs in Nepal. Their careers began with the salt trade between Tibet and India, but today they have spread into all spheres of contemporary life - including construction, politics, business, academia, arts and literature.

The secret of this expansion is the *dighur* system. A group of friends or relatives pool a given amount of money, sometimes thousands of rupees each, and give the whole sum

every year to one among them. The recipient uses the lean as he sees fit; whether he loses or gains money is his own affair, and his only obligation is to feed the *dighur*. When everyone in the pool has taken a turn, the *dighur* is automatically dissolved. An interesting self-financing device based on mutual trust, the system does away with interest rates and presupposes stability of currency.

A good example of Thakali behavioural patterns can be seen in the village of Marpha in the shadow of the Annapurna Himal. A casual glance at this community shows a strong sense of organization, discipline, cleanliness and far-sighted vision. Marpha is

Left, a homemade ferris wheel is part of village festival celebrations. **Above**, a Buddhist child is protected with sacred strings.

picturesquely wedged between steep sandstone cliffs on one side and a small ledge of cultivated fields overlooking the Kali Gandaki on the other. Along cobbled alleyways, whitewashed mud houses with flat roofs surround a succession of courtyards where livestock feed on fragrant juniper boughs, which the people also use to make tea. There is running water and a drainage system, an exceptional phenomenon in Nepal.

Most Thakalis are small farmers, growing barley and some potatoes. Savings are often invested in herds of yaks grazing the upper pastures. These long-haired Asiatic oxen are good providers; the females, *naks*, give milk; their cheese is sold as well as used for home

folk characterised by the high cheekbones of their northern heritage and live generally in central and western Nepal along the Kali Gandaki watershed. Farmers and herders, they cultivate maize, millet, mustard seeds and potatoes, that staple for survival in the hills. Cattle are kept and buffaloes provide meat, but sheep are of paramount importance for their wool and suitability to the middle hill grazing. Families own perhaps a dozen sheep, grouped in village flocks of 200 - 300. Four or five shepherds, accompanied by their fierce mastiff dogs, take them to the upper pastures from April to September, when the shearing is done. The flocks return to the village in October, for the important

consumption. The beasts' rough wool and hides are used in clothing, tents and pack saddles (see page 205).

People of the Middle Hills: The various peoples living in the temperate zone of Nepal's middle hills are sometimes erroneously referred to *en masse* as Gurkhas. The British and Indian armies have famed Gurkha regiments, named after the soldiers from the former Kingdom of Gorkha. But there is no single ethnic group today called Gurkha. By tradition, most Gurkha soldiers come from the Gurung, Magar, Rai, Limbu, Yakha and Sunuwar peoples of Nepal.

The Gurungs are self-sufficient hardy hill

Dasain festival when all the family gathers; then they head south for the winter, sometimes as far as the inner Terai hills. Wool is soaked and washed, but used undyed when woven in traditional patterns by Gurung women.

Magars are quite predominant numerically. They have earned a reputation for martial qualities both within and outside of Nepal, though they are basically self-sufficient hill peasants. They grow rice, maize, millet, wheat and potatoes, depending upon the suitability of the terrain they occupy. Spread out all over western and central Nepal, from the high Himalayan valleys to the plains of the Terai, the Magars, of Tibeto-Burman stock, have adopted whatever language, culture, religion, style of dress, and even architectural style is dictated by their area of settlement.

Rai, Limbu, Yakha and Sunuwar people of the eastern hills, like Magars and Gurungs, favour military service to all other professions, mainly because soldiers return home with added prestige and income. But the majority of them stay at home and practice subsistence agriculture. They are nominally Hindu, although some have adopted Buddhism or their own animistic practices in a unique melange typical of Nepalese religion.

Brahmans and Chhetris: The ubiquitous

derstood by outsiders. It was first instigated for social expediency by the early Malla rulers to protect their regime. Most societies in the world have hierarchical systems based both on birth and pedigree as well as wealth and position, groups with whom they prefer to socialize and intermarry, and groups whom they consider different. Hinduism merely institutionalises this concept.

In Nepal, the Hindu caste system socially, occupationally and ritually defines all people by the group into which they are born. It is elaborated into a number of rules for eating, marrying, working and touching. But as strong and persuasive as this system is, Nepal is unique in the Hindu world for the

Brahmans and Chhetris, along with the occupational castes of Nepal, have also traditionally played an important role in Nepalese society. Originally from west Nepal, the majority have a preference for the temperate middle hills, although they have dispersed in all parts of the Terai.

Orthodox Hindus, they believe in a hierarchical caste structure. "Caste", a word originally brought to Nepal and the Indian subcontinent by the Portuguese, is easily misun-

Left, three Newar girls from the Kathmandu Valley. **Above**, ornate jewellery is characteristic of Tamang women.

degree to which economic, political and romantic deviations from the caste norms are accepted and incorporated into society.

Brahmans and Chhetris are, like their neighbouring ethnic groups, predominantly subsistence farmers. However, the literary and priestly tradition of the Brahmans has facilitated their taking important roles in modern Nepalese government, education and business.

Similarly, most of the ruling families, including the famous Ranas, have been drawn from the Chhetri caste. The distinguished Thakuris are also Chhetris, but they claim to have come from Rajasthan in contrast to the rest of the clan who originally migrated eastward into Nepal.

Together, the Brahmans and Chhetris have provided the *lingua franca*, Nepali, and the main cultural and legal framework for Nepal's national identity.

Peoples of the Terai: The Terai Hindus, especially the high caste peoples, are more orthodox and conservative than the hill people. Although the caste system has lost is legal support, the higher castes still control most of the region's wealth and carry considerable political clout. Movement across the India-Nepal border is unrestricted, especially for marriages and socio-economic relations, thus cementing caste ties.

Villages are clusters of 30 to 100 or more dwellings, built with bamboo walls plastered with cow dung and mud, and topped by thatched or tile roofs. Concrete walls and cement roofs are signs of wealth.

Lowland ethnic groups such as the Tharu, Danuwar, Majhi and Darai live along the northern strip of eastern Terai and throughout western Terai. Rajbansi, Satar, Dhimal and Bodo peoples live in the far eastern districts of Jhapa and Morang. Moslems are found along the central and western sections of the Terai.

Numbering about half a million people, Tharu are among the most ancient people in-habiting the Terai, and are made up of several distinct groups with different customs. The eradication of malaria in the 1950s and the land reforms of the 1960s pushed waves of hill people to settle in the Terai. Some Tharu moved away, like the Dangaura who migrated to Karnali in far west Nepal; others stayed, such as the Mahaton and Nawalpuria in the Chitwan Valley, and now live alongside other Nepalese ethnic groups.

Tharu villages are easy to recognize, being scattered and, in some cases, very picturesque clustered villages. Their spacious longhouses, with mud and latticework walls decorated with animal and fish designs, are protected from the sun by wide, sloping, grass roofs. If the means of subsistence are sufficient, these longhouses can be occupied by families of as many as 150 people. With small doorways, the huge halls inside are divided into rooms by rows of the typical Tharu silos, moulded by the women and used for grain storage.

In most areas, their agriculture is stationary but primitive; Tharu maintain traditional irrigation systems and cultivate rice, maize, wheat and barley in the rich Terai land. They keep chickens and ducks, breed a few pigs, goats, and buffalos, and fish the big rivers by throwing jute nets. Fish, shrimps and snails are an important part of their diet, eaten daily with rice. They collect wild berries and medicinal herbs from the jungle, and occasionally hunt small animals such as porcupines or bamboo rats.

The bejewelled Tharu women usually marry early, though their life does not change much until they give birth. Their lovers must often work for their parents-in-law, sometimes for two or three years before they "earn" the right to marry. Age defines authority in the family; the old man is the overlord and the mother or elder sister rules over the female side of the household.

Living as they do in the realm of tigers, crocodiles and scorpions, Tharu venerate animistic spirits of the forest, as well as some Hindu deities. A village goddess is worshipped by each community at a small simple shrine, tended by their own priests or *gurwas*.

Above, Brahman with *tika* and topi. **Right**, cremation at Pashupatinath on the Bagmati River.

GURKHAS: BRAVEST OF THE BRAVE

Rare is the person today who has not heard of the Gurkha soldiers, the brave troops from Nepal's isolated hills who bolster the forces of the British and Indian armies.

Famed for their tenacity and loyalty in warfare since the late 18th century, these *khukri*-wielding soldiers underscored their fame by playing a key role in the 1982 Falkland Islands crisis.

The original Gurkha troops were from Gorkha, the small principality in central Nepal from which Prithvi Narayan Shah conquered the Kathmandu Valley in 1769 and unified the land of Nepal. Composed largely of Thakuri, Magar and Gurung men, these forces by 1814 had swept their long *khukris* across the central Himalaya.

The first two regular Gorkhali battalions were raised in 1763. Known as the Sri Nath and Purano Gorakh, they fought together against the British in 1769, and saw separate action against Tibet and in the Anglo-Nepal war of 1814-1816. It was the Anglo-Nepal war that first thrust the legend of Gurkha bravery into Western minds.

Impressed by what they had seen, the British East India Company began recruiting Gurkhas into their service. Gurkha recruitment was not formalised by the British until 1886, but by that time, India already had eight Gurkha Rifles units. Most of the men were drawn from the Magar and Gurung tribes, but others came from the Rais, Limbus and Sunuwars of the eastern hills and from the Khasas of the west.

At first, given their past hostilities, the relationship between the British and Nepalis was uneasy. By the time of the emergence of the Rana regime in 1846 and the subsequent visit to England of Jung Bahadur Rana, there was no question of the Gurkhas' allegiance. During the Indian mutiny of 1857, the British Gurkha regiments were joined by 12,000 of Jung Bahadur's own troops, with decisive results.

Over the nest 50 years, the Gurkhas fought all over south Asia, from Afghanistan to Malaya and even as far afield as African Somaliland in 1903. And when they were not fighting, they were climbing mountains. Long before the Sherpas had achieved fame as guides and mountaineers, Gurkhas were climbing many western Himalayan peaks.

In the Alps of Europe in 1894, a pair of Gurkhas named Amar Singh Thapa and Karbir Burathoki travelled 1,600 kilometers (1,000 miles) in 86 days, crossing 39 passes and scaling 21 peaks. They named a Swiss

peak Piz Gurkha after being the first to climb its 3,063 meters (10,049 feet); a nearby col was named Gurkha Pass. In 1907, Burathoki and Englishman Tom Longstaff accomplished the first major ascent of a Himalayan peak, Trisul (7,120 meters or 23,360 feet). Gurkhas were involved in five Everest expeditions between 1921 and 1937.

The World Wars: But war beckoned the Gurkhas to new destinations. With the advent of the First World War, they were called on in even greater numbers. More than 114,000 Gurkhas were called into active service in Givenchy, Ypres, Gallipolli, Palestine, Mesopotamia, Suez, Persia and

Left, traditional *khukri* knife is an integral part of a Gurkha's uniform. **Above**, *"Bravest of the brave, most generous of the generous, never had country more faithful friends than you"*.

Waziristan. Another 200,000 men were mobilized in the Indian army. Two Gurkhas - Kulbir Thapa (France, 1915) and Karna Bahadur Rana (Palestine, 1918) were awarded the Victoria Cross for gallantry.

In the Second World War, Gurkha strength was expanded to 45 battalions. These soldiers saw action in Iraq, Persia, Cyprus, Tunisia, Italy, Greece, Burma, Malaya and Indonesia; ten Victoria Crosses were awarded. Two of the battalions were paratroopers.

As the tale is told today, the British were seeking volunteers in a Gurkha regiment for a risky 1,000 foot airdrop behind enemy lines. About half of the troops stepped for-

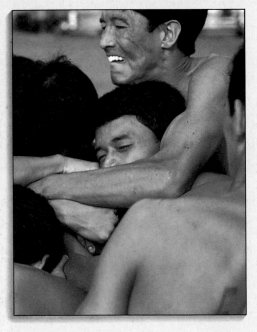

ward. The regiment leader proceeded to explain the troops' role in the drop, when a surprised voice queried: "Oh, you mean we can use parachutes?" Every remaining Gurkha promptly volunteered.

Two years after the Second World War ended, with the granting of independence to India, the Gurkha regiments were divided. Six of the ten regiments became the Indian Gurkha Rifles; the remaining four - the 2nd, 6th, 7th and 10th - remained the British Brigade of Gurkhas. In India, the troops plunged immediately into the India-Pakistan conflict over Kashmir; later came the Sino-Indian war of 1962 and further battles between

India and Pakistan in 1965 and 1971.

The British Brigade served in Malaya, Indonesia, Brunei and Cyprus. Another Victoria Cross, the 13th awarded to a Gurkha soldier, was presented to Lance Corporal Ram Bahadur Limbu for heroism in the face of overwhelming odds in Sarawak in 1965.

Gurkha soldiers are recruited as teenagers of 17 or 18 from their villages. There are recruiting depots at Pokhara in west Nepal and at Dharan in the east. Strict medical tests limit enlistment; those who succeed are provided with uniforms and good food, and are flown to Hong Kong for ten months of schooling and basic training. Then they have their first home leave, and their villages invariably treat them as heros.

Many Nepalese spend their entire working careers in the Gurkhas. It is a position of great status, and an important earner of foreign exchange for the country of Nepal. Only tourism in fact earns more. Gurkha salaries, pensions and related services provide a significant contribution to the economy.

Gurkhas today man posts in Hong Kong, Singapore, Brunei and Belize in Central America. But it was the South Atlantic skirmish between Britain and Argentina that brought them back into the public eye.

Perhaps the Gurkhas' ire was raised by the Argentine press, which belittled them as a cross between dwarfs and mountain goats. Perhaps the long sea voyage from the British Isles made them anxious to expend extra energy ashore; Gurkhas are notoriously bad sailors, and rely heavily on seasickness pills for travel between ports. Or perhaps the curry and rice diet which provides their daily sustenance gave them an emotional lift. Whichever, their action in the Falklands added another chapter to their legend.

Argentine troops guarding Port Stanley may have heard rumours about *khukri* decapitations of troops opposing the Gurkhas in other campaigns. For as the Gurkhas advanced on Argentine positions, the South American troops "turned and fled", according to a British newspaper report. The British Broadcasting Corporation reported that "the Argentines dropped their rifles and abandoned mortars and machine guns."

Above, competition to be selected to become a Gurkha soldier is intense. **Right**, physical and medical records are tested and checked.

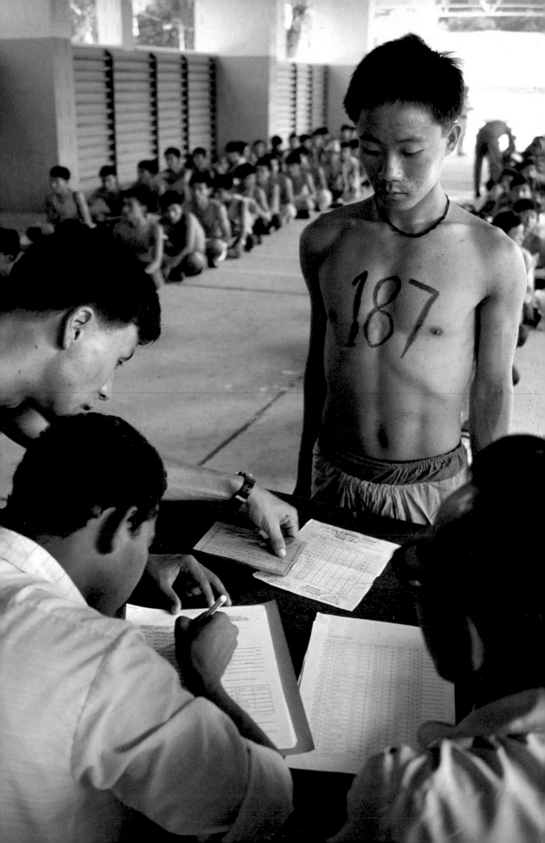